West's Law School Advisory Board

JESSE H. CHOPER

Professor of Law, University of California, Berkeley

DAVID P. CURRIE

Professor of Law, University of Chicago

YALE KAMISAR

Professor of Law, University of Michigan Professor of Law, University of San Diego

MARY KAY KANE

Chancellor, Dean and Distinguished Professor of Law, University of California, Hastings College of the Law

WAYNE R. LaFAVE

Professor of Law, University of Illinois

ARTHUR R. MILLER

Professor of Law, Harvard University

GRANT S. NELSON

Professor of Law, University of California, Los Angeles

JAMES J. WHITE

Professor of Law, University of Michigan